SCHOLASTIC

2

Math Problem-Solving Packets

Mini-Lessons for the Interactive Whiteboard With Reproducible Packets That Target and Teach Must-Know Math Skills

Carole Greenes, Carol Findell & Mary Cavanagh

NEW YORK • TORONTO • LONDON • AUCKLAND • SYDNEY
MEXICO CITY • NEW DELHI • HONG KONG • BUENOS AIRES

Teaching *Resources*

Editor: Maria L. Chang
Cover design by Jorge J. Namerow
Interior design by Melinda Belter
Illustrations by Teresa Anderko

ISBN: 978-0-545-45953-2
Copyright © 2012, 2008 by Carole Greenes, Carol Findell, and Mary Cavanagh
All rights reserved.
Printed in the U.S.A.

1 2 3 4 5 6 7 8 9 10   40   19 18 17 16 15 14 13 12

Table of Contents

Introduction

Welcome to *Math Problem-Solving Packets: Grade 2.* This book is designed to help you introduce children to problem-solving strategies and give them practice in essential number concepts and skills, while motivating them to write and talk about big ideas in mathematics. It also builds the foundation for more advanced math learning—algebra, in particular—in the upper grades.

Building Key Math Skills

The National Council of Teachers of Mathematics (NCTM) identifies problem solving as a key process skill and considers the teaching of strategies and methods of reasoning to solve problems a major part of the mathematics curriculum for children of all ages. The Common Core State Standards (CCSS) concurs. "Make sense of problems and persevere in solving them" is the first standard for Mathematical Practice in CCSS.

The problem-solving model first described by renowned mathematician George Polya in 1957 provides the framework for the problem-solving focus of this book. All the problems contained here require children to interpret data displays—such as text, charts, diagrams, graphs, pictures, and tables—and answer questions about them. As they work on the problems, children learn and practice the following problem-solving strategies:

- making lists or cases of possible solutions and testing those solutions
- identifying, describing, and generalizing patterns
- working backward
- reasoning logically
- reasoning proportionally

As children solve the problems in this book, they'll also practice counting, computing, applying concepts of place value and number theory, reasoning about the magnitudes of numbers, and more. In addition, they will learn the "language of mathematics," which includes terminology (e.g., *odd number, variable*) as well as symbols (e.g., $>$, $<$). Children will see the language in the problems and illustrations and use the language as they discuss and write about how they solve the problems.

How to Use This Book

This book contains six problem-solving packets—each composed of nine problems featuring the same type of data display (e.g., diagrams, scales, and arrays of numbers)—that focus on one or more problem-solving strategies and algebraic concepts. Each set opens with an overview of the type of problems/tasks in the set, the problem-solving focus, the number concepts or skills needed to solve the problems, the CCSS standard(s) covered, the math language emphasized in the problems, and guiding questions to be used with the first two problems of the packet to help children grasp the key concepts and strategies.

The first two problems in each packet are designed to be discussed and solved in a whole-class setting. The first, "Solve the Problem," introduces children to the type of display and problem they will encounter in the packet. You may want to have children work on this first problem individually or in pairs before you engage in any formal instruction. Encourage children to wrestle with the problem and come up with some strategies they might use to solve it. Then gather children together and use the guiding questions provided to help them discover key mathematical relationships and understand the special vocabulary used in the problem. This whole-class discussion will enhance student understanding of the problem-solving strategies and math concepts featured in the packet.

The second problem, "Make the Case," uses a multiple-choice format. Three different characters offer possible solutions to the problem. Children have to determine which character—Señorita Rita, Granny Knot, or Ms. Yogi—has the correct answer. Before they can identify the correct solution, children have to solve the problem themselves and analyze each of the responses. Invite them to speculate about why the other two characters got the wrong answers. (Note: Although we offer a rationale for each wrong answer, other explanations are possible.) As they justify their choices in the "Make the Case" problems, children gain practice and confidence in using math language.

While working on these first two problems, encourage children to talk about their observations and hypotheses. This talk provides a window into what children do and do not understand. Working on "Solve the Problem" and "Make the Case" should take approximately one math period.

The remaining problems in each packet are sequenced by difficulty. They all feature a series of questions that involve analyzing the data display. In the first three or four problems of each set, problem-solving "guru" Ima Thinker provides hints about how to begin solving the problems. The rest of the problems offer no hints. If children have difficulty solving these latter problems, you might want to write "Ima" hints for each of them or ask children to develop hints before beginning to solve the problems. An answer key is provided at the back of the book.

The problem-solving packets are independent of one another and may be used in any order and incorporated into the regular mathematics curriculum at whatever point makes sense. We recommend that you work with each packet in its entirety before moving on to the next one. Once you and your students work through the first two problems, you can assign problems 1 through 7 for children to do on their own or in pairs. You may wish to have them complete the problems during class or for homework.

Using the CD

In addition to the reproducible problem-solving packets in this book, you'll find a CD with ActivInspire (Promethean) files* and PDFs of "Solve the Problem," "Make the Case," and "Solve It" problems, for use on the interactive whiteboard. (Black-line masters of these pages also appear in the book.) Display "Solve the Problem" and "Make the Case" on the whiteboard to help you in leading a whole-class discussion of the problems. Then use the additional "Solve It" problems to guide children in applying our three-step problem-solving process:

1. **Look:** What is the problem? What information do you have? What information do you need?
2. **Plan and Do:** How will you solve the problem? What strategies will you use? What will you do first? What's the next step? What comes after that?
3. **Answer and Check:** What is the answer? How can you be sure that your answer is correct?

These "Solve It" problems encourage writing about mathematics and may be used at any time. They are particularly effective as culminating activities for the problem-solving packets.

*If you do not have ActivInspire software on your computer, click on the folder titled **Promethean Installers**. To install the software on a Mac, double-click on **ActivInspire_v1.6.43277_USA.dmg** file, then click on **ActivInspire.mpkg**. If you have a PC, double-click on **ActivInspireSuite_v1.6.43277_en_US_setup_PC.exe**. Please read the PDF file for the license agreement.

The problem-solving packets in this book support the following Common Core State Standards.

MATHEMATICAL PRACTICES
1. Make sense of problems and persevere in solving them.
2. Reason abstractly and quantitatively.
3. Construct viable arguments and critique the reasoning of others.
4. Model with mathematics.
5. Use appropriate tools strategically.
6. Attend to precision.
7. Look for and make use of structure.
8. Look for and express regularity in repeated reasoning.

OPERATIONS AND ALGEBRAIC THINKING
Represent and solve problems involving addition and subtraction.
2.OA.1 Use addition and subtraction within 100 to solve one- and two-step word problems involving situations of adding to, taking from, putting together, taking apart, and comparing, with unknowns in all positions, e.g., by using drawings and equations with a symbol for the unknown number to represent the problem.

Add and subtract within 20.
2.OA.2 Fluently add and subtract within 20 using mental strategies. By end of Grade 2, know from memory all sums of two one-digit numbers.

Work with equal groups of objects to gain foundations for multiplication.
2.OA.3 Determine whether a group of objects (up to 20) has an odd or even number of members, e.g., by pairing objects or counting them by 2s; write an equation to express an even number as a sum of two equal addends.
2.OA.4 Use addition to find the total number of objects arranged in rectangular arrays with up to 5 rows and up to 5 columns; write an equation to express the total as a sum of equal addends.

NUMBER AND OPERATIONS IN BASE TEN
Use place value understanding and properties of operations to add and subtract.
2.NBT.5 Fluently add and subtract within 100 using strategies based on place value, properties of operations, and/or the relationship between addition and subtraction.
2.NBT.6 Add up to four two-digit numbers using strategies based on place value and properties of operations.
2.NBT.9 Explain why addition and subtraction strategies work, using place value and the properties of operations.

References

Common Core State Standards Initiative. (2010). *Common core state standards for mathematics.* Washington, DC: National Governors Association Center for Best Practices and the Council of Chief State School Officers.

Greenes, Carole, Mary Cavanagh, Linda Dacey, Carol Findell, & Marian Small. (2001). *Navigating through algebra in grades pre-kindergarten–grade 2.* Reston, VA: National Council of Teachers of Mathematics.

Greenes, Carole, & Carol Findell. (Eds.). (2005). *Developing students' algebraic reasoning abilities.* (Vol. 3 in the NCSM Monograph Series). Boston, MA: Houghton Mifflin.

Greenes, Carole, & Carol Findell. (2005). *Groundworks: Algebraic thinking.* Chicago: Wright Group/McGraw Hill.

Moses, Barbara. (Ed.). (1999). *Algebraic thinking, grades K–12: Readings from NCTM's school-based journals and other publications.* Reston, VA: National Council of Teachers of Mathematics.

National Council of Teachers of Mathematics. (2000). *Principles and standards for school mathematics.* Reston, VA: National Council of Teachers of Mathematics.

Polya, George. (1957). *How to solve it.* Princeton, NJ: Princeton University Press.

Small, Marian, Linda Sheffield, Mary Cavanagh, Linda Dacey, Carol Findell, & Carole Greenes. (2004). *Navigating through problem solving and reasoning in grade 2.* Reston, VA: National Council of Teachers of Mathematics.

Usiskin, Zalman. (1997). Doing algebra in grades K–4. *Teaching Children Mathematics. 3*(6), 346–356.

How Old Am I?

Overview

Children use clues to interpret age relationships among animals and work backward through the clues to answer the questions.

Problem-Solving Strategies

- Work backward
- Use logical reasoning

Related Math Skills

- Compare ages and numbers
- Add
- Subtract

Algebra Focus

- Represent quantitative relationships
- Write and solve equations

CCSS Correlations

2.OA.1 • 2.OA.2

Math Language

- Greatest number
- How old?
- Least number
- Months
- Older than, oldest
- Years
- Younger than, youngest

Introducing the Packet

Make photocopies of "Solve the Problem: How Old Am I?" (page 11) and distribute to children. Have children work in pairs, encouraging them to discuss strategies they might use to solve the problem. You may want to walk around and listen in on some of their discussions. After a few minutes, display the problem on the interactive whiteboard (see the CD) and use the following questions to guide a whole-class discussion on how to solve the problem:

- What did Ima do first to figure out the ages? *(She matched the least number to the youngest cat.)*

- Which cat is the youngest? *(Mouser)*

- How old is Mouser? *(3 years old)*

- Which cat's age can you figure out next? *(Fancy)*

- Why can't you figure out Rocky's age before finding Fancy's age? *(One fact states that Rocky is 3 years older than Fancy, so we have to figure out Fancy's age before we can figure out Rocky's age.)*

Work together as a class to answer the questions in "Solve the Problem: How Old Am I?"

Math Chat With "Make the Case"

Display "Make the Case: How Old Am I?" on the interactive whiteboard. Before children can decide which character's "nose knows," they need to figure out the answer to the problem. Encourage children to work in pairs to solve the problem. Then bring the class together for another whole-class discussion. Ask:

- Who has the right answer? *(Señorita Rita)*

- What do you think Señorita Rita did first to solve the problem? *(She chose the least number and matched it with Dash because he is the youngest. So Dash is 2 years old.)*

- What did Señorita Rita do next? *(She added 2 + 4 to get Lucky's age. Lucky is 6 years old.)*

- How did Señorita Rita find the ages for Spike and Chase? *(Spike is one year younger than Lucky, or 6 – 1 = 5 years old, and Chase is three years older than Lucky, or 5 + 3 = 8 years old.)*

- How do you think Granny Knot got her answer? *(She might have thought that the first clue said, "I am 3 years old." She didn't read the whole sentence.)*

- How do you think Ms. Yogi got her answer? *(She might have added 3 to the least age: 2 + 3 = 5.)*

Name _____ Date _____

SOLVE THE PROBLEM

How old are the cats?

Screech — I am 1 year younger than Rocky.

I am 1 year older than Mouser. — **Fancy**

Rocky — I am 4 years older than Fancy.

I am the youngest.

Mouser

CATS' AGES

4   7   8   3

I'll start with Mouser. Her age is the least number.

Ima Thinker

1. Mouser is _____ years old.

2. Fancy is _____ years old.

3. Rocky is _____ years old.

4. Screech is _____ year old.

5. Rocky is _____ years older than Mouser.

Name _____ Date _____

MAKE THE CASE

How old is Chase?

Chase

I am 3 years older than Spike.

I am 4 years older than Dash.

Lucky

Spike

I am 1 year younger than Lucky.

I am the youngest.

Dash

RABBITS' AGES

| 6 | 5 | 2 | 8 |

I'm certain that Chase is 8 years old.

Granny Knot

Chase is definitely 3 years old.

Señorita Rita

No way. Chase is 5 years old.

Whose nose knows?

Ms. Yogi

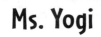

Name _____ Date _____

PROBLEM 1

How old are the bears?

Boxy

I am 2 years older than Sleepy.

I am 5 years older than Gus.

Scoop

Sleepy

I am Scoop's twin.

I am the youngest.

Gus

BEARS' AGES

8   3   8   10

I'll start with Gus. His age is the least number.

Ima Thinker

1. Gus is _____ years old.

2. Scoop is _____ years old.

3. Sleepy is _____ years old.

4. Boxy is _____ years old.

5. Boxy is _____ years older than Gus.

13

PROBLEM 2

How old are the hippos?

Lola

I am 7 years older than Hoofer.

I am 3 years older than Dippy.

Blossom

I am 2 years younger than Blossom.

I am the youngest.

Dippy

Hoofer

HIPPOS' AGES

5	13	8	6

I'll start with Dippy. His age is the least number.

Ima Thinker

1. Dippy is _____ years old.

2. Blossom is _____ years old.

3. Hoofer is _____ years old.

4. Lola is _____ years old.

5. Lola is _____ years older than Dippy.

Name _____ Date _____

PROBLEM 3

How old are the horses?

Swifty

I am 5 years younger than Thunder.

I am 3 years younger than Lolly.

Chops

Thunder

I am 2 years older than Chops.

I am the oldest.

Lolly

HORSES' AGES

6   8   9   3

I'll start with Lolly. Her age is the greatest number.

Ima Thinker

1. Lolly is _____ years old.

2. Chops is _____ years old.

3. Thunder is _____ years old.

4. Swifty is _____ years old.

5. Swifty is _____ years younger than Lolly.

PROBLEM 4

How old are the lions?

King

I am 1 year younger than Specs.

I am 6 years younger than Leo.

Lady

Specs

I am 3 years older than Lady.

I am the oldest.

Leo

LIONS' AGES

| 5 | 4 | 8 | 2 |

I'll start with Leo. His age is the greatest number.

Ima Thinker

1. Leo is _____ years old.

2. Lady is _____ years old.

3. Specs is _____ years old.

4. King is _____ years old.

5. King is _____ years younger than Leo.

16

Name _____ Date _____

PROBLEM
5

How old are the penguins?

Tux

I am 10 years older than Scruffy.

I am 8 years younger than Star.

Pebbles

I am 6 years younger than Pebbles.

I am the oldest.

Scruffy

Star

PENGUINS' AGES

10   18   4   14

1. Star is _____ years old.

2. Pebbles is _____ years old.

3. Scruffy is _____ years old.

4. Tux is _____ years old.

5. Tux is _____ years younger than Star.

17

PROBLEM
6

How old are the camels?

Lumpy

I am 4 years older than Chuckles.

I am 10 years younger than Tut.

Lola

I am 20 years younger than Lola.

I am the oldest.

Chuckles

Tut

CAMELS' AGES

12	42	32	16

1. Tut is _____ years old.

2. Lola is _____ years old.

3. Chuckles is _____ years old.

4. Lumpy is _____ years old.

5. Lumpy is _____ years younger than Tut.

Name _____ Date _____

PROBLEM 7

How old are the gorillas?

Kong

I am 13 years younger than Kiki.

I am 20 years younger than Digit.

Zola

Kiki

I am 15 years older than Zola.

I am the oldest.

Digit

GORILLAS' AGES

35	30	17	15

1. Digit is _____ years old.

2. Zola is _____ years old.

3. Kiki is _____ years old.

4. Kong is _____ years old.

5. Kong is _____ years younger than Digit.

Number on a Hat

Overview

Presented with clues, children make a list of numbers and try to identify the value of a variable.

Problem-Solving Strategies

- Make lists of possible solutions based on clues
- Use clues to eliminate unlikely solutions
- Use logical reasoning

Related Math Skills

- Compare numbers
- Identify tens and ones digits of numbers
- Skip count
- Add
- Measurement relationships: number of days in a week, inches in a foot, pennies in a dime

Algebra Focus

- Represent unknowns with letters
- Interpret mathematical relationships

CCSS Correlations

2.OA.1 • 2.OA.2 • 2.OA.3

Math Language

- Between
- Even number, odd number
- Digit
- Less than
- Greater than
- Count by 2s, 3s, 5s, and 10s
- Square

Introducing the Packet

Make photocopies of "Solve the Problem: Number on a Hat" (page 22) and distribute to children. Have children work in pairs, encouraging them to discuss strategies they might use to solve the problem. You may want to walk around and listen in on some of their discussions. After a few minutes, display the problem on the interactive whiteboard (see the CD) and use the following questions to guide a whole-class discussion on how to solve the problem:

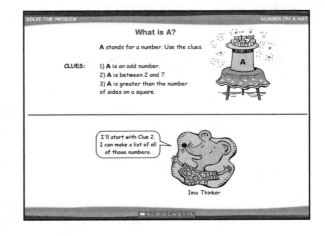

- Why did Ima start with Clue 2? *(Clue 2 says A is between 2 and 7. Only four numbers fit this clue.)*

- What numbers are on Ima's list based on Clue 2? *(3, 4, 5, and 6)*

- Which clue do you think Ima will use next? *(Clue 1. From that clue, Ima can cross off the numbers 4 and 6.)*

- Could Ima have used Clue 3 instead of Clue 1 as the second clue? *(Yes. Clue 3 would eliminate the numbers 3 and 4.)*

- How many sides does a square have? *(4)*

Work together as a class to answer the questions in "Solve the Problem: Number on a Hat."

Math Chat With "Make the Case"

Display "Make the Case: Number on a Hat" on the interactive whiteboard. Before children can decide which character's "nose knows," they need to figure out the answer to the problem. Encourage children to work in pairs to solve the problem. Then bring the class together for another whole-class discussion. Ask:

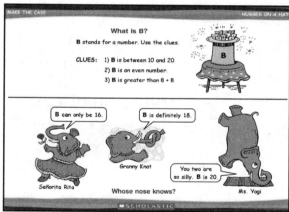

- Who has the right answer? *(Granny Knot)*

- How did you figure it out? *(Starting with Clue 1, list the numbers 11 through 19. From Clue 2, cross off all odd numbers. That leaves 12, 14, 16, and 18. From Clue 3, cross off everything except 18. B is 18.)*

- How do you think Señorita Rita got the answer of 16? *(She might have thought that Clue 3 said that B was 8 + 8, not that B was greater than 8 + 8.)*

- How do you think Ms. Yogi got the answer of 20? *(She might have thought that numbers between 10 and 20 included 10 and 20, and 20 is greater than 18.)*

Name _____ Date _____

SOLVE THE PROBLEM

What is A?

A stands for a number.
Use the clues.

CLUES:

1) **A** is an odd number.

2) **A** is between 2 and 7.

3) **A** is greater than the number of sides on a square.

I'll start with Clue 2. I can make a list of all of those numbers.

Ima Thinker

1. Write the numbers on Ima's list. _____

2. Look at Clue 1.
   What numbers can you cross off the list? _____

3. Look at Clue 3.
   What number can you cross off the list now? _____

4. What is **A**? _____

Name _____ Date _____

MAKE THE CASE

What is B?

B stands for a number.
Use the clues.

CLUES:

1) **B** is between 10 and 20.
2) **B** is an even number.
3) **B** is greater than 8 + 8.

Granny Knot

B is definitely 18.

B can only be 16.

You two are so silly. **B** is 20.

Señorita Rita

Whose nose knows?

Ms. Yogi

PROBLEM
1

What is C?

C stands for a number.
Use the clues.

CLUES:

1) **C** is a number you say when you count by 3s.

2) **C** is an even number.

3) **C** is less than the number of days in a week.

I'll start with Clue 3. I can make a list of those numbers.

Ima Thinker

1. Write the numbers on Ima's list. _____

2. Look at Clue 1.
   What numbers can you cross off the list? _____

3. Look at Clue 2.
   What number can you cross off the list now? _____

4. What is **C**? _____

PROBLEM 2

What is D?

D stands for a number.
Use the clues.

CLUES:

1) **D** is a number you say when you count by 2s.

2) **D** is less than 15.

3) **D** is greater than the number of inches in a foot.

I'll start with Clue 2. I can make a list of all of those numbers.

Ima Thinker

1. Write the numbers on Ima's list. _____

2. Look at Clue 1.
   What numbers can you cross off the list? _____

3. Look at Clue 3.
   What numbers can you cross off the list now? _____

4. What is **D**? _____

PROBLEM 3

What is E?

E stands for a number.
Use the clues.

CLUES:

1) **E** is between 20 and 35.

2) Both digits of **E** are odd numbers.

3) **E** has two digits that are the same.

I'll start with Clue 1. I can make a list of all those numbers.

Ima Thinker

1. Write the numbers on Ima's list. _____

2. Look at Clue 2.
   What numbers can you cross off the list? _____

3. Look at Clue 3.
   What number can you cross off the list now?_____

4. What is **E**? _____

Name _____ Date _____

PROBLEM
4

What is F?

F stands for a number.
Use the clues.

CLUES:

1) **F** is less than 40.

2) You say **F** when you count by 5s.

3) **F** is greater than 30.

I'll start with Clue 1. It will help me know the greatest number on my list.

Ima Thinker

1. What is the greatest number on Ima's list? _____

2. Which clue gives the least number for the list? _____

   What is the least number on the list? _____

3. Look at Clue 2.
   What numbers can you cross off the list? _____

4. What is **F**? _____

PROBLEM 5

What is G?

G stands for a number.
Use the clues.

CLUES:

1) **G** is less than 30.

2) The ones digit of **G** is greater than 4 + 3.

3) The tens digit is an even number.

4) When you add the digits of **G**, the sum is an even number.

1. Which clue will you use first? _____

2. When you use that clue, what numbers will be on your list?

   _____

3. What is **G**? _____

4. How did you figure out the number for **G**?

   _____

   _____

Name _____   Date _____

PROBLEM
6

What is H?

H stands for a number.
Use the clues.

CLUES:

1) **H** is a number you say when you
count by 2s.

2) **H** is less than the number of pennies
equal to 3 dimes.

3) **H** is greater than 12 + 12.

4) When you add the digits of **H**, the sum is less than 10.

1. Which clue will you use first? _____

2. When you use that clue, what numbers will be on your list?

_____

3. What is **H**? _____

4. How did you figure out the number for **H**?

_____

_____

Name _____ Date _____

PROBLEM
7

What is J?

J stands for a number.
Use the clues.

CLUES:

1) **J** is greater than 70.

2) **J** is a 2-digit number.

3) The ones digit of **J** is greater than its tens digit.

4) When you add the digits of **J**, the sum is greater than 16.

1. Which clue will you use first? _____

2. When you use that clue, what numbers will be on your list?

   _____

3. What is **J**? _____

4. How did you figure out the number for **J**?

   _____

   _____

Polka Dots

Overview

Given one item with a specified number of dots, children draw the same number of dots on each similar item and identify the total number of dots.

Problem-Solving Strategy

Draw pictures to solve problems

Related Math Skills

• Add with more than two addends
• Count by 2s, 3s, 4s, 5s, 6s, and 10s
• Relate division to multiplication

Algebra Focus

Reason about proportional relationships

CCSS Correlations

2.OA.1 • 2.OA.3 • 2.OA.4

Math Language

• How many?
• In all

Introducing the Packet

Make photocopies of "Solve the Problem: Polka Dots" (page 33) and distribute to children. Have children work in pairs, encouraging them to discuss strategies they might use to solve the problem. You may want to walk around and listen in on some of their discussions. After a few minutes, display the problem on the interactive whiteboard (see the CD) and use the following questions to guide a whole-class discussion on how to solve the problem:

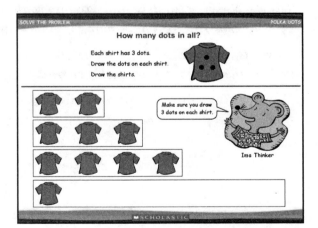

• Look at the picture of the shirt on the top of the page. How many polka dots are on the shirt? *(3)*

• What are the words next to the shirt? *(Each shirt has 3 dots.)*

• What do you need to do? *(Draw 3 dots on each shirt. Then tell the number of dots in all.)*

- What do you see in the picture for question 1? *(Two shirts with no dots)*

- What will you do first? *(Draw 3 dots on each shirt.)*

- How many dots will there be in all? *(6)*

- How can you figure out the number of dots in all on 3 shirts? *(Count by 3s: 3, 6, 9. There are 9 dots. Or, add 3 + 3 + 3 = 9.)*

Work together as a class to answer the questions in "Solve the Problem: Polka Dots."

Math Chat With "Make the Case"

Display "Make the Case: Polka Dots" on the interactive whiteboard. Before children can decide which character's "nose knows," they need to figure out the answer to the problem. Encourage children to work in pairs to solve the problem. Then bring the class together for another whole-class discussion. Ask:

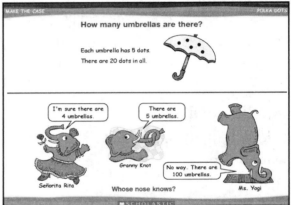

- Who has the right answer? *(Señorita Rita)*

- How did you figure it out? *(Since one umbrella has 5 dots, then 4 umbrellas have 5 + 5 + 5 + 5, or 20 dots. You can also count by 5s: 5, 10, 15, 20. That's four 5s, so there are 4 umbrellas.)*

- How do you think Granny Knot got the answer 5? *(Maybe she just used the number 5 because there are 5 dots on each umbrella.)*

- How do you think Ms. Yogi got the answer 100? *(She may have thought that 20 is the number of umbrellas and counted by 5s saying 20 numbers; the 20th number is 100.)*

Name _____ Date _____

SOLVE THE PROBLEM

How many dots in all?

Each shirt has 3 dots.

Draw the dots on each shirt.

Draw the shirts.

Make sure you draw 3 dots on each shirt.

Ima Thinker

1. 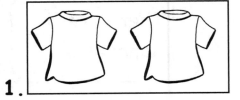 _____ shirts
_____ dots in all

2.  _____ shirts
_____ dots in all

3.  _____ shirts
_____ dots in all

4.  _____ shirts
18 dots in all

Name _____   Date _____

MAKE THE CASE

How many umbrellas are there?

Each umbrella has 5 dots.

There are 20 dots in all.

I'm sure there are 4 umbrellas.

There are 5 umbrellas.

Granny Knot

No way. There are 100 umbrellas.

Señorita Rita

Whose nose knows?

Ms. Yogi

Name _____ Date _____

PROBLEM 1

How many dots in all?

Each hat has 2 dots.

Draw the dots on each hat.

Draw the hats.

Make sure you draw 2 dots on each hat.

Ima Thinker

1.
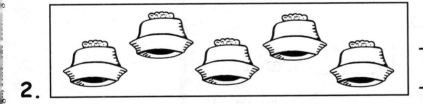
_____ hats

_____ dots in all

2.
_____ hats

_____ dots in all

3.
_____ hats

_____ dots in all

4.
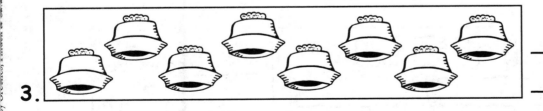
_____ hats

_20_ dots in all

Name _____   Date _____

PROBLEM 2

How many dots in all?

Each scarf has 4 dots.

Draw the dots on each scarf.

Draw the scarves.

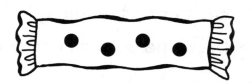

Make sure you draw 4 dots on each scarf.

Ima Thinker

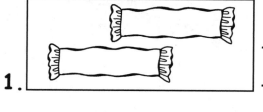

1. _____ scarves

_____ dots in all

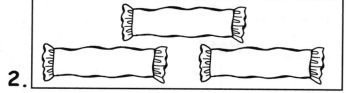

2. _____ scarves

_____ dots in all

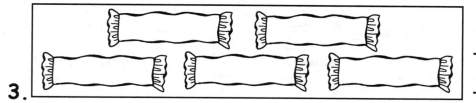

3. _____ scarves

_____ dots in all

4. _____ scarves

<u>24</u> dots in all

Name _____ Date _____

PROBLEM 3

How many dots in all?

Each skirt has 6 dots.

Draw the dots on each skirt.

Draw the skirts.

Make sure to draw 6 dots on each skirt.

Ima Thinker

1. ____ skirts

____ dots in all

2. ____ skirts

____ dots in all

3. ____ skirts

____ dots in all

4. ____ skirts

<u>36</u> dots in all

Math Problem-Solving Packets: Grade 2 © 2012 by Greenes, Findell & Cavanagh, Scholastic Teaching Resources

Name _____ Date _____

PROBLEM
4

How many dots in all?

Each bow tie has 4 dots.

Draw the dots on each bow tie.

Draw the bow ties.

Make sure to draw 4 dots on each bow tie.

Ima Thinker

1. ____ bow ties
   ____ dots in all

2. ____ bow ties
   ____ dots in all

3. ____ bow ties
   ____ dots in all

4. ____ bow ties
   _28_ dots in all

38

PROBLEM
5

How many dots in all?

Each sweater has 10 dots.

Draw the dots on each sweater.

Draw the sweaters.

1. _____ sweaters

_____ dots in all

2. _____ sweaters

_____ dots in all

3. _____ sweaters

_70_ dots in all

4. _____ sweaters

_100_ dots in all

Name _____ Date _____

PROBLEM 6

How many dots in all?

Each jacket has 5 dots.

Draw the dots on each jacket.

Draw the jackets.

1.    ____ jackets
   ____ dots in all

2.    ____ jackets
   ____ dots in all

3. ____ jackets
   _35_ dots in all

4. ____ jackets
   _45_ dots in all

Name _____ Date _____

PROBLEM
7

How many dots in all?

Each coat has 3 dots.

Draw the dots on each coat.

Draw the coat.

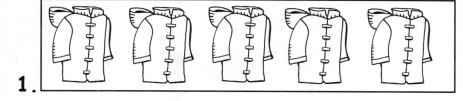

1. _____ coats

_____ dots in all

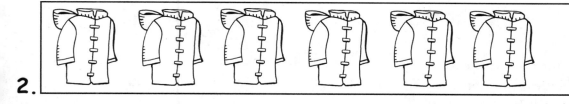

2. _____ coats

_____ dots in all

3. _____ coats

__24__ dots in all

4. _____ coats

__36__ dots in all

Weird Robots

Overview
Presented with patterns on robots with various features—such as arms, teeth, eyes, and more—children identify the relationship between the robot number and the number of features.

Problem-Solving Strategies
- Make drawings
- Generalize patterns

Related Math Skills
- Skip count by 2s, 3s, 4s, 5s
- Identify odd and even numbers
- Add

Algebra Focus
- Identify and continue patterns
- Identify the relationship between the robot number and the number of items on the robot

CCSS Correlations
2.OA.1 • 2.OA.2 • 2.OA.3

Math Language
- How many?
- Pattern

Introducing the Packet
Make photocopies of "Solve the Problem: Weird Robots" (page 44) and distribute to children. Have children work in pairs, encouraging them to discuss strategies they might use to solve the problem. You may want to walk around and listen in on some of their discussions. After a few minutes, display the problem on the interactive whiteboard (see the CD) and use the following questions to guide a whole-class discussion on how to solve the problem:

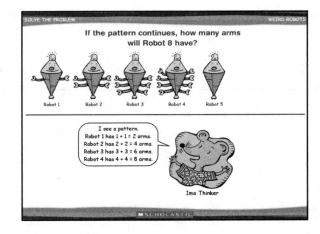

- How many arms on Robot 1? *(2)* on Robot 2? *(4)* on Robot 3? *(6)*

- What pattern does Ima see? *(The numbers of arms are numbers you say when you count by 2s. The number of arms on a robot is double the robot number. Robot 1 has 1 + 1, or 2 arms, and Robot 2 has 2 + 2, or 4 arms.)*

- If the pattern continued, how many arms would Robot 6 have? *(12)*

- How many arms would Robot 8 have? *(16)*

- Which robot would have 14 arms? *(Robot 7)* How do you know? *(7 + 7 = 14)*

- Which robot would have 20 arms? *(Robot 10)* How do you know? *(10 + 10 = 20)*

Work together as a class to answer the questions in "Solve the Problem: Weird Robots."

Math Chat With "Make the Case"

Display "Make the Case: Weird Robots" on the interactive whiteboard. Before children can decide which character's "nose knows," they need to figure out the answer to the problem. Encourage children to work in pairs to solve the problem. Then bring the class together for another whole-class discussion. Ask:

- Who has the right answer? *(Granny Knot)*

- How did you figure it out? *(The number of teeth on a robot is double the number of the robot before it. For Robot 7, the number of teeth is double 6, or 6 + 6 = 12.)*

- How do you think Señorita Rita got the answer of 14? *(She might have doubled the robot number; 7 + 7 = 14.)*

- How do you think Ms. Yogi got the answer of 10? *(She might have doubled the number for Robot 5 instead of Robot 6; 5 + 5 = 10.)*

Name _____ Date _____

SOLVE THE PROBLEM

If the pattern continues, how many arms will Robot 8 have?

| Robot 1 | Robot 2 | Robot 3 | Robot 4 | Robot 5 |

I see a pattern.
Robot 1 has 1 + 1 = 2 arms.
Robot 2 has 2 + 2 = 4 arms.
Robot 3 has 3 + 3 = 6 arms.
Robot 4 has 4 + 4 = 8 arms.

Ima Thinker

1. Draw the arms on Robot 5.

2. How many arms are on Robot 5? _____

3. How many arms are on Robot 6? _____

4. How many arms are on Robot 8? _____

5. Which Robot has 20 arms? _____

MAKE THE CASE

If the pattern continues, how many teeth will Robot 7 have?

Robot 1   Robot 2   Robot 3   Robot 4   Robot 5

Robot 7 will have 14 teeth.

Robot 7 will have 12 teeth. I'm sure of it!

Granny Knot

Señorita Rita

You're both wrong. Robot 7 will have 10 teeth.

Ms. Yogi

Whose nose knows?

45

Name _____ Date _____

PROBLEM 1

If the pattern continues, how many flowers will be on Robot 7's hat?

Robot 1   Robot 2   Robot 3   Robot 4   Robot 5

I see a pattern.
Robot 1 has 0 flowers.
Robot 2 has 1 flower.
Robot 3 has 2 flowers.
Robot 4 has 3 flowers.

Ima Thinker

1. Draw the flowers on Robot 5's hat.

2. How many flowers will be on Robot 5's hat? _____

3. How many flowers will be on Robot 6's hat? _____

4. How many flowers will be on Robot 7's hat? _____

PROBLEM 2

If the pattern continues, how many eyes will Robot 7 have?

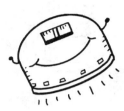

Robot 1   **Robot 2**   **Robot 3**   **Robot 4**   **Robot 5**

I see a pattern.
Robot 1 has 2 eyes.
Robot 2 has 3 eyes.
Robot 3 has 4 eyes.
Robot 4 has 5 eyes.

Ima Thinker

1. Draw the eyes on Robot 5.

2. How many eyes will be on Robot 5? _____

3. How many eyes will be on Robot 6? _____

4. How many eyes will be on Robot 7? _____

Name _____ Date _____

PROBLEM 3

If the pattern continues, how many feet will Robot 8 have?

Robot 1   **Robot 2**   **Robot 3**   **Robot 4**   **Robot 5**

I see a pattern.
Robot 1 has 1 foot.
Robot 2 has 3 feet.
Robot 3 has 5 feet.
Robot 4 has 7 feet.

Ima Thinker

1. Draw the feet on Robot 5.

2. How many feet will be on Robot 6? _____

3. How many feet will be on Robot 7? _____

4. How many feet will be on Robot 8? _____

PROBLEM 4

If the pattern continues, how many hairs will Robot 10 have?

 **Robot 1**    **Robot 2**    **Robot 3**    **Robot 4**

I see a pattern.
Robot 1 has 3 hairs.
Robot 2 has 4 hairs.
Robot 3 has 5 hairs.
Robot 4 has 6 hairs.

Ima Thinker

1. How many hairs will be on Robot 5? _____

2. How many hairs will be on Robot 7? _____

3. How many hairs will be on Robot 10? _____

4. Which robot will have 20 hairs? _____

Name _____ Date _____

PROBLEM
5

If the pattern continues, . . .

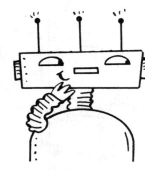   

Robot 1   Robot 2   Robot 3   Robot 4

1. How many antennas will be on Robot 5? _____

2. How many antennas will be on Robot 6? _____

3. How many antennas will be on Robot 8? _____

4. Which robot will have 30 antennas? _____

Name _____   Date _____

PROBLEM 6

If the pattern continues, . . .

Robot 1   Robot 2   Robot 3   Robot 4

1. How many spots will be on Robot 5? _____

2. How many spots will be on Robot 6? _____

3. How many spots will be on Robot 7? _____

4. Which robot will have 50 spots? _____

Name _____ Date _____

PROBLEM 7

If the pattern continues, . . .

Robot 1

Robot 2

Robot 3

Robot 4

1. How many buttons will Robot 5 have? _____

2. How many buttons will Robot 6 have? _____

3. How many buttons will Robot 8 have? _____

4. Which robot will have 21 buttons? _____

Face Value

Overview

Clues are given in the form of two equations with two unknowns (faces). Children figure out the values of the unknowns.

Problem-Solving Strategies

• Reason deductively
• Test values

Related Math Skills

• Add with one- and two-digit numbers
• Subtract with one- and two-digit numbers

Algebra Focus

• Solve for the values of two unknowns
• Replace unknowns with their values

CCSS Correlations

2.OA.1 • 2.OA.2

Math Language

• Equation
• Same numbers
• Stand for numbers

Introducing the Packet

Make photocopies of "Solve the Problem: Face Value" (page 55) and distribute to children. Have children work in pairs, encouraging them to discuss strategies they might use to solve the problem. You may want to walk around and listen in on some of their discussions. After a few minutes, display the problem on the interactive whiteboard (see the CD) and use the following questions to guide a whole-class discussion on how to solve the problem:

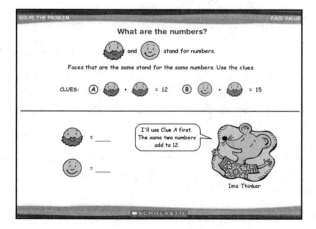

• Look at Clue A. What do you see? (*Two faces that are the same. Each face stands for the same number. The sum of the two numbers is 12.*)

- Look at Clue B. What do you see? *(Two different faces. The two numbers the faces stand for add up to 15.)*

- Why did Ima start with Clue A? *(Both faces are the same, so each face must stand for 6.)*

- If the face with a beard stands for 6, how can you figure out the number of the face without a beard? *(In Equation B, replace the bearded face with 6. The face without a beard must then be 9. 6 + 9 = 15.)*

- Look at question 4. How can you figure out the sum? *(Replace each face with its number and then add: 6 + 6 + 9 = 21.)*

- How can you figure out the answer to question 5? *(Replace each face card with its number; 6 + 6 − 9 = 3.)*

Work together as a class to answer the questions in "Solve the Problem: Face Value."

Math Chat With "Make the Case"

Display "Make the Case: Face Value" on the interactive whiteboard. Before children can decide which character's "nose knows," they need to figure out the answer to the problem. Encourage children to work in pairs to solve the problem. Then bring the class together for another whole-class discussion. Ask:

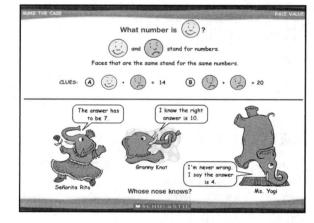

- Who has the right answer? *(Ms. Yogi)*

- How did you figure it out? *(Clue B shows that* ☹ + ☹ *= 20, so a sad face stands for 10. In Clue A, replace the sad face with 10. So* ☺ *+ 10 = 14; the smile face is 14 − 10 = 4.)*

- How do you think Granny Knot got the answer of 10? *(She might have mistakenly given the number for the sad face.)*

- How do you think Señorita Rita got the answer of 7? *(She might have mistakenly thought that both of the faces in Clue A had the same values; half of 14 is 7.)*

Name _____ Date _____

SOLVE THE PROBLEM

What are the numbers?

 and stand for numbers.

Faces that are the same stand for the same numbers. Use the clues.

CLUES:

A. 🧔 + 🧔 = 12

B. 😊 + 🧔 = 15

1. 🧔 = _____

2. 😊 = _____

3. 😊 + 😊 = _____

4. 🧔 + 🧔 + 😊 = _____

5. 🧔 + 🧔 – 😊 = _____

I'll use Clue A first. The same two numbers add to 12.

Ima Thinker

Name _____ Date _____

MAKE THE CASE

What number is ?

 and stand for numbers.

Faces that are the same stand for the same numbers. Use the clues.

CLUES:

A. **+** (sad face) **= 14**

B. (sad face) **+** (sad face) **= 20**

The answer has to be 7.

I know the right answer is 10.

Granny Knot

I'm never wrong. I say the answer is 4.

Señorita Rita

Whose nose knows?

Ms. Yogi

Name _____ Date _____

PROBLEM 1

What are the numbers?

 and stand for numbers.

Faces that are the same stand for the same numbers. Use the clues.

CLUES:

A. + = 6

B. + = 2

I'll use Clue B first. The same two numbers add to 2.

Ima Thinker

1.  = _____

2. = _____

3. + = _____

4.  + + = _____

5. + + = _____

Name _____ Date _____

PROBLEM 2

What are the numbers?

 and stand for numbers.

Faces that are the same stand for the same numbers. Use the clues.

CLUES:

A.  + = 4

B. + = 10

I'll use Clue A first. The same two numbers add to 4.

Ima Thinker

1. = _____

2.  = _____

3. + = _____

4.  – = _____

5. 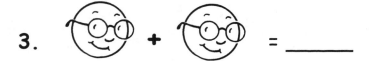 + + = _____

Name _____ Date _____

PROBLEM 3

What are the numbers?

 and stand for numbers.

Faces that are the same stand for the same numbers. Use the clues.

CLUES:

A.  **+**  **= 14**

B.  **–** **= 4**

I'll use Clue A first. The same two numbers add to 14.

Ima Thinker

1.  = _____

2. 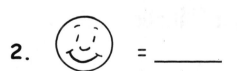 = _____

3.  **+**  = _____

4. 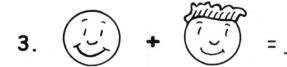 = _____

5.  = _____

59

Name _____ Date _____

PROBLEM 4

What are the numbers?

 and stand for numbers.

Faces that are the same stand for the same numbers. Use the clues.

CLUES:

A.  = 6

B. = 18

I'll use Clue B first. The same two numbers add to 18.

Ima Thinker

1. = _____

2. = _____

3. = _____

4.  = _____

5.  = _____

Name _____ Date _____

PROBLEM
5

What are the numbers?

 and stand for numbers.

Faces that are the same stand for the same numbers. Use the clues.

CLUES:

A.  **+** (face) = 24

B. (face) **−** (face) = 5

1. (face) = _____

2. (face) = _____

3. (face) **+** (face) **+** (face) = _____

4. (face) **+** (face) **+** (face) = _____

5. (face) **+** (face) **+** (face) **−** (face) = _____

Name _____ Date _____

PROBLEM
6

What are the numbers?

 and  stand for numbers.

Faces that are the same stand for the same numbers. Use the clues.

CLUES:

A.  + +  = 15

B. + = 25

1. = _____

2. = _____

3. − = _____

4. + + = _____

5. − − + = _____

Name _____ Date _____

PROBLEM 7

What are the numbers?

 and stand for numbers.

Faces that are the same stand for the same numbers. Use the clues.

CLUES:

A. − = 2

B. + + = 30

1. = _____

2. = _____

3. + + = _____

4. + − = _____

5. + + − = _____

Snack Bags

Overview
Clues are given in the form of two bags, each showing the total cost of different types of snacks. Children solve for the cost of each snack.

Problem-Solving Strategies
- Reason deductively
- Test values

Related Math Skills
- Add
- Subtract
- Find half of a number

Algebra Focus
- Solve for the values of two unknowns
- Replace unknowns with their values

CCSS Correlations
2.OA.1 • 2.OA.2 • 2.OA.3
2.NBT.5 • 2.NBT.6 • 2.NBT.9

Math Language
- ¢ (cents symbol)
- Cost
- Cost the same

Introducing the Packet
Make photocopies of "Solve the Problem: Snack Bags" (page 66) and distribute to children. Have children work in pairs, encouraging them to discuss strategies they might use to solve the problem. You may want to walk around and listen in on some of their discussions. After a few minutes, display the problem on the interactive whiteboard (see the CD) and use the following questions to guide a whole-class discussion on how to solve the problem:

- Look at the two bags. What is in the bag with two snacks? *(One pretzel and one apple juice)*

- What is in the bag with one snack? *(Apple juice)*

- Which cost can you figure out first? *(Apple juice)* Why? *(It is the only item in the bag.)*

- How much is the apple juice? *(15¢)*

- How can knowing that the apple juice is 15¢ help you figure out the cost of the pretzel? *(We can subtract the cost of the apple juice from the total cost; 25¢ – 15¢ = 10¢. The pretzel costs 10¢.)*

Work together as a class to answer the questions in "Solve the Problem: Snack Bags."

Math Chat With "Make the Case"

Display "Make the Case: Snack Bags" on the interactive whiteboard. Before children can decide which character's "nose knows," they need to figure out the answer to the problem. Encourage children to work in pairs to solve the problem. Then bring the class together for another whole-class discussion. Ask:

- Who has the right answer? *(Ms. Yogi)*

- How did you figure it out? *(Two cheese sticks cost 10¢. So one cheese stick is half of 10¢, or 5¢. The crackers are 14¢ – 5¢, or 9¢.)*

- How do you think Granny Knot got the answer of 7¢? *(She might have thought that since there are two items in the bag for 14¢, that each item costs the same; half of 14¢ is 7¢.)*

- How do you think Señorita Rita got the answer of 5¢? *(She might have mistakenly given the cost of the cheese stick instead of the crackers.)*

Name _____ Date _____

How much does each snack bag cost?

25¢

pretzel and apple juice

15¢

apple juice

Snacks that are the same cost the same.

I know the apple juice is 15¢. So, a pretzel + 15¢ = 25¢.

Ima Thinker

1.

pretzel

2.

2 pretzels

3.

2 apple juices and 1 pretzel

4.

2 apple juices and 2 pretzels

Name _____ Date _____

MAKE THE CASE

How much do the crackers cost?

10¢

2 cheese sticks

14¢

crackers and 1 cheese stick

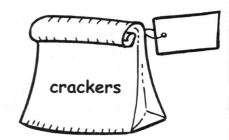

crackers

Snacks that are the same cost the same.

The crackers have to cost 5¢.

That's easy. The crackers cost 7¢.

Granny Knot

Señorita Rita

You're both wrong. The crackers cost 9¢.

Whose nose knows?

Ms. Yogi

Name _____   Date _____

PROBLEM 1

How much does each snack bag cost?

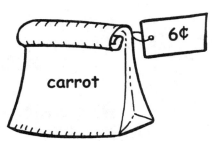

6¢

carrot

14¢

carrot and granola bar

Snacks that are the same cost the same.

I know the carrot is 6¢. So a granola bar + 6¢ = 14¢.

Ima Thinker

1.

granola bar

3.

2 carrots and granola bar

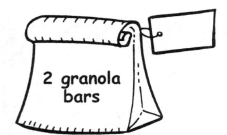

2.

2 granola bars

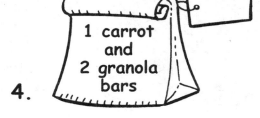

4.

1 carrot and 2 granola bars

68

Name _____ Date _____

PROBLEM 2

How much does each snack bag cost?

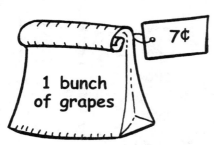

7¢

1 bunch of grapes

11¢

1 bunch of grapes and 1 strawberry

Snacks that are the same cost the same.

I know the grapes are 7¢. So a strawberry + 7¢ = 11¢.

Ima Thinker

1.

strawberry

2. 2 bunches of grapes and 1 strawberry

3.

1 bunch of grapes and 2 strawberries

4. 2 bunches of grapes and 2 strawberries

Name _____   Date _____

**PROBLEM
3**

How much does each snack bag cost?

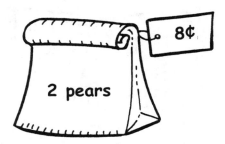

8¢

2 pears

16¢

pear
and a juice
box

Snacks that are the same cost the same.

I'll find the cost of one pear first. Then I'll find the cost of the juice box.

Ima Thinker

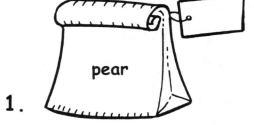

pear

1.

pear
and 2 juice
boxes

3.

juice box

2.

2 pears
and 2 juice
boxes

4.

Name _____ Date _____

PROBLEM
4

How much does each snack bag cost?

plum and banana — 22¢

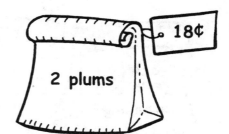

2 plums — 18¢

Snacks that are the same cost the same.

I'll figure out the cost
of one plum first.
Then I'll find the cost
of the banana.

Ima Thinker

1.

plum

2.

banana

3.

banana and 2 plums

4.

plum and 2 bananas

Name _____   Date _____

PROBLEM
5

How much does each snack bag cost?

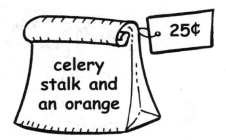

celery
stalk and
an orange

25¢

3 celery
stalks

15¢

Snacks that are the same cost the same.

1.

celery
stalk

3.

2 celery
stalks and
2 oranges

2.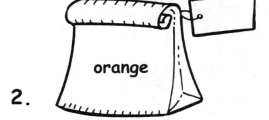

orange

4.

3 oranges
and
1 celery
stalk

Name _____   Date _____

PROBLEM
6

How much does each snack bag cost?

3 cherries   12¢

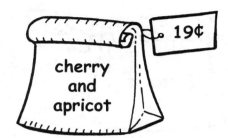

cherry
and
apricot   19¢

Snacks that are the same cost the same.

1.

cherry

3.

cherry
and
2 apricots

2.

apricot

4.

3 cherries
and
2 apricots

Name _____ Date _____

PROBLEM
7

How much does each snack bag cost?

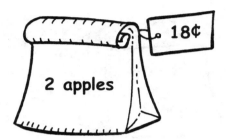

Snacks that are the same cost the same.

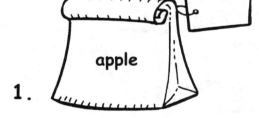

1.

3.

2.

4.

1. Look   What is the problem?

2. Plan and Do   What will you do first? How will you solve the problem?

3. Answer and Check   How can you be sure your answer is correct?

How old are the mice?

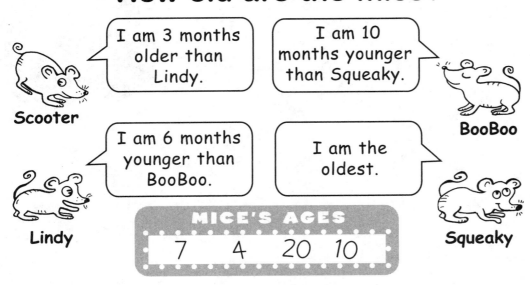

Scooter: I am 3 months older than Lindy.

BooBoo: I am 10 months younger than Squeaky.

Lindy: I am 6 months younger than BooBoo.

Squeaky: I am the oldest.

MICE'S AGES

7   4   20   10

SOLVE IT: NUMBER ON A HAT

What is Z?

Z stands for a number. Use the clues.

CLUES:

1) **Z** is a number you say when you count by 10s.

2) **Z** is between 20 and 60.

3) Both of **Z**'s digits are even numbers.

How many vests are there?

Each vest has 4 dots.

There are 32 dots in all.

SOLVE IT: WEIRD ROBOTS

If the pattern continues, which robot will have 28 stars?

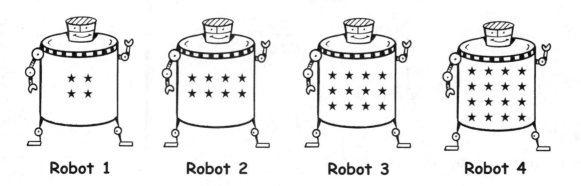

| Robot 1 | Robot 2 | Robot 3 | Robot 4 |

SOLVE IT: FACE VALUE

What number does the face with no ears stand for?

 and stand for numbers.

Faces that are the same stand for the same numbers.

CLUES:

A. (face) + (face) = 8

B. (face) + (face) = 10

SOLVE IT: SNACK BAGS

How much does this snack bag cost?

1 yogurt and 1 pepper

2 peppers and 1 yogurt   46¢

2 peppers   16¢

Snacks that are the same cost the same.

ANSWER KEY

How Old Am I?
(pages 11–19)
Solve the Problem
1. 3
2. 4
3. 8
4. 7
5. 5

Make the Case
Whose nose knows?
Señorita Rita

Problem 1
1. 3
2. 8
3. 8
4. 10
5. 7

Problem 2
1. 5
2. 8
3. 6
4. 13
5. 8

Problem 3
1. 9
2. 6
3. 8
4. 3
5. 6

Problem 4
1. 8
2. 2
3. 5
4. 4
5. 4

Problem 5
1. 18
2. 10
3. 4
4. 14
5. 4

Problem 6
1. 42
2. 32
3. 12
4. 16
5. 26

Problem 7
1. 35
2. 15
3. 30
4. 17
5. 18

Solve It: How Old Am I?
1. **Look:** Four mice give facts about their ages. A sign shows the ages in months.
2. **Plan and Do:** Work backward. Squeaky is the oldest so he is 20 months old. BooBoo is 10 months younger than Squeaky, so BooBoo is 20 − 10, or 10 months old. Lindy is 6 months younger than BooBoo, so Lindy is 10 − 6, or 4 months old. Scooter is 3 months older than Lindy, so Scooter is 4 + 3, or 7 months old.
3. **Answer and Check:** Squeaky is 20, BooBoo is 10, Lindy is 4, and Scooter is 7 months old. Check answers with clues. 20 − 10 is 10; 10 − 6 is 4; 4 + 3 is 7.

Number on a Hat
(pages 22–30)
Solve the Problem
1. 3, 4, 5, 6
2. 4 and 6
3. 3
4. 5

Make the Case
Whose nose knows? Granny Knot

Problem 1
1. 0, 1, 2, 3, 4, 5, 6
2. 0, 1, 2, 4, 5
3. 3
4. 6

Problem 2
1. 0, 1, 2, 3, . . . , 13, 14
2. 0, 1, 3, 5, 7, 9, 11, 13
3. 2, 4, 6, 8, 10, 12
4. 14

Problem 3
1. 21, 22, 23, . . . , 33, 34
2. 21, 22, . . . , 30, 32, 34
3. 31
4. 33

Problem 4
1. 39
2. Clue 3; 31
3. 31, 32, 33, 34, 36, 37, 38, 39
4. 35

Problem 5
1. Clue 1
2. 1, 2, 3, . . . , 28, 29
3. 28
4. Clue 1 gives 1 to 29. From

Clue 3 we know that G is a 2-digit number and that the tens digit is 2. That leaves 21, 22, . . . , 28, 29. From Clue 2 we are left with only 28 and 29. Only 28 fits Clue 4.

Problem 6
1. Clue 2
2. 1, 2, . . . , 28, 29
3. 26
4. From Clue 2, H is 1, 2, . . . , 28, 29. Then Clue 3 eliminates the numbers 1 to 24. Clue 4 then eliminates 28 and 29. Clue 1 eliminates 25 and 27. So H is 26.

Problem 7
1. Clue 2
2. 10, 11, . . . , 98, 99
3. 89
4. From Clue 2, the numbers are 10 to 99. Clue 1 eliminates all but 71 to 99. Clue 3 leaves only 78, 79, and 89. Only 89 fits Clue 4.

Solve It: Number on a Hat
1. **Look:** There are 3 clues about the number Z. The clues have to be used to figure out Z.
2. **Plan and Do:** Choose the clue to use first. Clue 2 identifies the numbers 21 through 59. Make a list of those numbers. Clue 1 eliminates all numbers except for 30, 40, and 50. Clue 3 eliminates 30 and 50. Z is 40.
3. **Answer and Check:** 40. Check 40 with the clues. Clue 1: You say the number 40 when you count by 10s. Clue 2: 40 is between 20 and 60. Clue 3: 40 has two even digits. The answer checks.

Polka Dots (pages 33–41)
1. 2 shirts, 6 dots in all
2. 3 shirts, 9 dots in all
3. 4 shirts, 12 dots in all
4. 6 shirts, 18 dots in all

Make the Case
Whose nose knows?
Señorita Rita

Problem 1
1. 3 hats, 6 dots in all
2. 5 hats, 10 dots in all
3. 8 hats, 16 dots in all
4. 10 hats, 20 dots in all

Problem 2
1. 2 scarves, 8 dots in all
2. 3 scarves, 12 dots in all
3. 5 scarves, 20 dots in all
4. 6 scarves, 24 dots in all

Problem 3
1. 2 skirts, 12 dots in all
2. 3 skirts, 18 dots in all
3. 4 skirts, 24 dots in all
4. 6 skirts, 36 dots in all

Problem 4
1. 3 bow ties, 12 dots in all
2. 5 bow ties, 20 dots in all
3. 6 bow ties, 24 dots in all
4. 7 bow ties, 28 dots in all

Problem 5
1. 4 sweaters, 40 dots in all
2. 6 sweaters, 60 dots in all
3. 7 sweaters, 70 dots in all
4. 10 sweaters, 100 dots in all

Problem 6
1. 3 jackets, 15 dots in all
2. 6 jackets, 30 dots in all
3. 7 jackets, 35 dots in all
4. 9 jackets, 45 dots in all

Problem 7
1. 5 coats, 15 dots in all
2. 6 coats, 18 dots in all
3. 8 coats, 24 dots in all
4. 12 coats, 36 dots in all

Solve It: Polka Dots
1. **Look:** There is a picture of one vest with 4 polka dots. The problem is to figure out the number of vests that have 32 polka dots in all.
2. **Plan and Do:** One vest has 4 dots. To figure out the number of vests that have 32 dots in all, count up by 4s to 32. Record the number of numbers you say.
3. **Answer and Check:** 8 vests in all. Figure out the number of dots on 4 vests (4 + 4 + 4 + 4 = 16), and then add 16 + 16 to get the number of dots on 8 vests.

Weird Robots (pages 44–52)
1. Draw 10 arms on Robot 5.
2. 10 arms
3. 12 arms
4. 16 arms
5. Robot 10

Make the Case
Whose nose knows?
Granny Knot

Problem 1
1. Draw 4 flowers on Robot 5's hat.
2. 4 flowers
3. 5 flowers
4. 6 flowers

Problem 2
1. Draw 6 eyes on Robot 5.
2. 6 eyes
3. 7 eyes
4. 8 eyes

Problem 3
1. Draw 9 feet on Robot 5.
2. 11 feet
3. 13 feet
4. 15 feet

Problem 4
1. 7 hairs
2. 9 hairs
3. 12 hairs
4. Robot 18

Problem 5
1. 15 antennas
2. 18 antennas
3. 24 antennas
4. Robot 10

Problem 6
1. 25 spots
2. 30 spots
3. 35 spots
4. Robot 10

Problem 7
1. 11 buttons
2. 13 buttons
3. 17 buttons
4. Robot 10

Solve It: Weird Robots
1. Look: Robots have stars. The numbers of stars are numbers you say when you count by 4s. The problem is to figure out which robot has 28 stars.
2. Plan and Do: The number of the robot is the same as the number of 4s that have to be added or counted to get 28 (4, 8, 12, 16, 20, 24, 28), or 28 stars.

3. Answer and Check: Robot 7. Check by adding seven 4s or counting up by 4s and saying seven numbers.

Face Value (page 55–63)
1. 6
2. 9
3. 18
4. 21
5. 3

Make the Case
Whose nose knows? Ms. Yogi

Problem 1
1. 1
2. 5
3. 10
4. 7
5. 11

Problem 2
1. 2
2. 8
3. 16
4. 6
5. 18

Problem 3
1. 7
2. 3
3. 10
4. 9
5. 17

Problem 4
1. 9
2. 3
3. 12
4. 21
5. 15

Problem 5
1. 12
2. 7
3. 21
4. 26
5. 24

Problem 6
1. 5
2. 20
3. 15
4. 45
5. 30

Problem 7
1. 10
2. 12
3. 32
4. 14
5. 20

Solve It: Face Value
1. Look: Two equations are shown with faces standing for numbers. Equation A shows two faces with big ears and a sum of 8. Equation B shows two different faces and a sum of 10. The equations have to be solved to figure out what number the face with no ears stands for.
2. Plan and Do: Use Equation A to find the value of the face with big ears, which is 4. Replace the face with big ears in Equation B with 4. Then the face with no ears is 10 – 4, or 6.
3. Answer and Check: 6; Replace the faces with their values in Equations A and B. The answers should check.

Snack Bags (pages 66–74)
1. 10¢
2. 20¢
3. 40¢
4. 50¢

Make the Case
Whose nose knows? Ms. Yogi

Problem 1
1. 8¢
2. 16¢
3. 20¢
4. 22¢

Problem 2
1. 4¢
2. 18¢
3. 15¢
4. 22¢

Problem 3
1. 4¢
2. 12¢
3. 28¢
4. 32¢

Problem 4
1. 9¢
2. 13¢
3. 31¢
4. 35¢

Problem 5
1. 5¢
2. 20¢
3. 50¢
4. 65¢

Problem 6
1. 4¢
2. 15¢
3. 34¢
4. 42¢

Problem 7
1. 9¢
2. 10¢
3. 29¢
4. 48¢

Solve It: Snack Bags
1. Look: Two bags. In the ba[g] for 46¢, there is one yogurt and 2 peppers. In the bag fo[r] 16¢, there are 2 peppers. Th[e] problem is to figure out the cost of a bag with one yogur[t] and one pepper.
2. Plan and Do: In the sec- ond bag there are only 2 pep- pers for 16¢, so one pepper [is] half of 16¢, or 8¢. In the firs[t] bag, the 2 peppers are 16¢, so the yogurt is 46¢ – 16¢, o[r] 30¢. So one yogurt and one pepper are 30¢ + 8¢, or 38¢.
3. Answer and Check: 38¢. T[o] check, replace the yogurt with 30¢ and each pepper with 8¢, and figure out the total cost of each bag. The total costs should match the number of cents on each bag's tag.